"All the President's Men and Women"

The Secretary of State
through
Warren Christopher

John Hamilton

Published by Abdo & Daughters, 4940 Viking Dr., Suite 622, Edina, MN 55435.

Library bound edition distributed by Rockbottom Books, Pentagon Tower, P.O. Box 36036, Minneapolis, Minnesota 55435.

Cover Photo by: Blackstar
Inside Photos by: The Bettmann Archive (17)
AP/Wide World Photos (5, 13, 24)
Archive Photos (8, 19)
Black Star (14, 21, 23, 27, 28)

Edited By: Sue L. Hamilton

Library of Congress Cataloging–in–Publication Data
Hamilton, John, 1959-
      The Secretary of State / written by John Hamilton
            p.   cm — (All the President's men and women)
      Includes bibliographical references and index.
      ISBN 1-56239-250-6 (lib. bdg.)
      1. United States. Dept. of State—Juvenile literature. 2. Foreign ministers—United States—Biography—Juvenile literature.
      [1. United States. Dept. of State. 2. Cabinet officers.]
      I. Title. II. Series.
JX1706.A4   1993
353.1—dc20   93-22623
                                                                            CIP
                                                                             AC

CONTENTS

The President's Cabinet: An Overview 4

The Secretary of State 6

History of the State Department 7

Other Responsibilities

      The United States Foreign Service 11

      National Security Council 12

      United Nations 14

      Travel Help 15

Biographies

      Thomas Jefferson 16

      George C. Marshall 18

      John Foster Dulles 20

      Henry Kissinger 22

      Warren Christopher 25

Glossary 29

Connect With Books 31

Index 32

The President's Cabinet: An Overview

When someone is elected President of the United States, he (or she) immediately takes on a huge amount of responsibility. Presidents must oversee all laws passed by Congress. They're the head of the armed forces. They must decide foreign policy—how should the U.S. help its friends and allies, and how should we punish our enemies? If the economy stumbles, the President must try to get it back on the right track. Presidents must make sure that laws are handed down fairly; energy is used wisely; parks and other government lands are put to proper use; citizens are educated, put to work, and kept healthy. And that is just a small part of what Presidents do!

Obviously, no one person, no matter how smart, can possibly know everything there is to know to do a President's job. A President paints in broad strokes, deciding the tone and direction of how the country should be run. To help with the details, the President has a "cabinet," a group of people to meet with regularly for advice on important decisions that must be made every day.

There's no law that says the President must have a cabinet. It's a system that has evolved by custom over the years. The United States Constitution says that the President "may require the opinion, in writing, of the principal officer in each of the executive departments, upon any subject relating to the duties of their respective offices." But the President doesn't have to ask their advice, and doesn't have to go along with what they say if the President thinks they are wrong.

The heads of these cabinet departments are called "secretaries" and are appointed by the President. The Senate checks the secretaries' backgrounds and votes on whether to accept them. Nominees are picked for their experience and special talents in the areas they are to oversee. Only rarely is a President's pick rejected. After the Senate accepts, or "confirms" cabinet secretaries, the President alone has the right to remove them if unhappy with the way they are performing their duties.

When a President resigns, or is defeated in an election, the entire cabinet also resigns. New Presidents can rehire old cabinet members, but they usually want their own trusted advisers to help them run the country.

This book will take a look at the oldest (and many say the most important) cabinet position, the **Secretary of State**.

President Clinton presides over his first Cabinet meeting in the Cabinet Room of the White House.

The Secretary of State

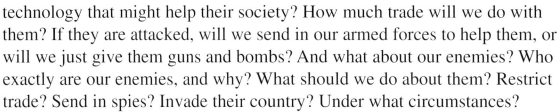

The Secretary of State is the head of the United States State Department. The Secretary of State helps the President decide how the United States will act toward foreign countries. This is called "foreign policy." How far will we go in helping our friends and allies? Should we give them loans, or new technology that might help their society? How much trade will we do with them? If they are attacked, will we send in our armed forces to help them, or will we just give them guns and bombs? And what about our enemies? Who exactly are our enemies, and why? What should we do about them? Restrict trade? Send in spies? Invade their country? Under what circumstances?

As you can see, the Secretary of State has a lot of questions that need answering. And the answers and advice the Secretary gives the President can have a huge impact on world affairs. President Eisenhower said that the Secretary of State's position was "the greatest and most important job in the world." Because we are a superpower, the way we treat another country can have a big effect on that country's society.

To keep the President up to date on what is happening around the world, the Secretary of State does a lot of traveling. Representing the United States in other countries, the Secretary of State talks with kings and queens, prime ministers, and other leaders (called "heads of state"). It's the Secretary's job to stay on good terms with these other countries, and to see how they feel about what the United States is doing in the world. After gathering this information, the Secretary reports back to the President on how we stand with our friends and enemies.

To get all the information it needs, the State Department is constantly talking with Congress, other U.S. Departments and agencies, foreign governments, and of course, the American people. To do all this work, and figure out the mountains of facts and opinions that pour in from these different sources, the State Department employs thousands of people in embassies around the world and in offices in Washington, D.C.

History of the State Department

The State Department has been around the longest of all the parts of the U.S. Government. Even before the Declaration of Independence was signed in 1776, our Founding Fathers knew how important is was to establish foreign affairs. Without good relations with other countries, the United States would have been very handicapped in its fight for freedom from Great Britain.

Benjamin Franklin was a great statesman, scientist and writer. He also traveled widely and knew how important it was to keep ties with foreign countries. Under his direction, our new government set up the Committee of Secret Correspondence in 1775. This secret committee, which represented the beginning of our State Department, was formed to take the American Colony's case to the rest of Europe and try to get their support in our struggle for freedom.

By 1777, after war with Britain had broken out, the committee was renamed the Committee for Foreign Affairs of the Second Continental Congress. Its first ambassadors were such great statesmen as Thomas Jefferson, John Adams, and of course, Benjamin Franklin. It was the effort of the Foreign Affairs Committee that got France to sign the treaty promising money and military help for the war. Without France's assistance, we may never have gained our independence from Great Britain.

Benjamin Franklin, great statesman, scientist, writer, and one of the founders of our State Department.

In 1781 our country formed the Articles of Confederation (a collection of independent states not as strongly tied together like today's United States). The Foreign Affairs Committee became the Department of Foreign Affairs. The Department was responsible for working with Great Britain to sign the peace treaty in 1783 that made our independence official. Soon afterwards, we sent diplomats to several other countries to establish official ties to our new nation.

The United States Constitution took effect in 1789. Congress soon set up the Department of State. Its head, the Secretary of State, reported directly to the President. Though the new Constitution gave the President sole responsibility for handling foreign affairs, one person couldn't possibly keep track of all the details involved. Because of this, the President relied heavily on the advice and recommendations of his Secretary of State—as he does to this day.

The President doesn't always have to take the advice of the Secretary of State, however. In fact, in modern times, the Secretary of State has often been overshadowed by other trusted aides and advisers to the President. For example, during Richard Nixon's first term as President, Secretary of State William Rogers was often less important than National Security Adviser Henry Kissinger. Foreign diplomats often chose to talk with Kissinger instead of Rogers, knowing that Kissinger was closer to the President. Still, the State Department is powerful and influential. In fact, during President Nixon's second term, he promoted Henry Kissinger to Secretary of State.

Over the years, the jobs handled by the Department of State have become more and more complicated, especially after the end of World War II. Before the war, it was easy for America to isolate itself because of the two great oceans separating it from the rest of the world. In World War II, though, air power became very important. The oceans were no longer a barrier. Thrust into a more active world role at the end of the war, America became a superpower. Communism started to become popular during this time as well. Communism brought with it a battle of values, both political and social.

It was the State Department's job to try and figure out how we would respond to this threat to democracy.

Also during this time, many new nations appeared, rising from the former colonies of Europe. At the same time, the great countries in Europe saw much of their power decreasing. In the United States, the State Department tried to find ways to help the new countries so that they would develop friendly relations with America. Deciding which countries would get humanitarian aid became a big part of the State Department's job.

Just as the President can't possibly know everything there is to know about every country, the Secretary of State needs assistance to keep him aware of what is going on in the world. To help him, there are five Assistant Secretaries of State, each of whom is responsible for a different section of the world. These include Europe; Africa; the American Hemisphere; East Asia and the Pacific; and the Near East and South Asia. Each Assistant Secretary reports to the Secretary of State on his or her region.

Other Responsibilities

As we saw earlier, the Department of State advises the President on matters of foreign policy. This simply means trying to figure out how to deal with other countries in a way that helps America's security and well-being in the long run. As part of this responsibility, the State Department has other areas it is in charge of also.

United States Foreign Service

The future of America depends a lot on how we get along with other countries. The relations we have with these other countries are conducted mainly by the United States Foreign Service. The Foreign Service is a system of embassies that we have in other countries. Our chief representative at each embassy is called an ambassador. As of April 1990, the United States had 144 embassies, nine missions, 71 consulates general, 26 consulates, one branch office, and 23 consular agencies throughout the world. The United States has an embassy in each country of which we have diplomatic relations. Each embassy is located in the capital city. They all report to the State Department on a huge amount of information learned in these foreign countries every day. They provide the Secretary of State and the President with much of the raw information they need to make foreign policy decisions.

Ambassadors have a very important job. They are the personal representatives of the President and report to him through the Secretary of State. In addition to giving information back home about their host countries, they are responsible for negotiating treaties, explaining United States policy to the other countries' leaders, and maintaining cordial relations with the leaders and their people.

If the United States breaks off diplomatic relations with a country, the ambassador is called home. In this case, we talk with the country through a neutral third nation. For example, for a time we had no direct diplomatic relations with Cuba. Instead, Cuba and the United States talked diplomatically to each other by passing messages through Switzerland. Recently, relations have improved somewhat, so America and Cuba exchanged representatives in order to have better communications. We still have not exchanged full ambassadors, however.

It can be very difficult to enter the foreign service. Applicants need to be college graduates, often with advanced degrees. Difficult tests are given to those wishing to enter. They require a good knowledge of language, history, and political science. But if you qualify, you enter one of the oldest and proudest traditions of public service. And if you work your way up the ladder through many years of good service, you may even get appointed ambassador by the President.

Not all who work their way up get to be ambassadors, though. Presidents often appoint outsiders to be their personal representatives in foreign countries. Presidents often feel more comfortable appointing friends to these important positions, people they can trust. Sometimes, though, this can backfire, since the person the President appoints may not have much experience. In this case, the State Department may have to rely on experienced foreign service officers to get the best information.

National Security Council

In addition to overseeing the foreign service, the Secretary of State has another important job as a member of the President's National Security Council. The National Security Council collects information on the military, domestic and foreign policy of the United States and advises the President if our security is at risk. It makes sure that the actions we take and treaties we sign with other countries don't hurt the United States.

The Security Council was formed by the National Security Act of 1947. After World War II, the world was in a great deal of tension because of the rise of Communism and the spread of nuclear weapons. This was called the

Cold War. Because of these tensions and feelings of insecurity, our country needed a single group that could give the President accurate and complete information at a moment's notice.

The National Security Council acts as a sort of pool of information. This lets all the other departments and agencies of our government act together in an easier, more useful way. And with all this information at hand, the council can be a very good way for the President to get accurate information on security matters. It helps find, to the best of the President's ability, important ways to make our country more secure and safe.

President Bush meets in the Oval Office at the White House to receive a briefing from the National Security Council.

In addition to the Secretary of State, the National Security Council's members include the President, Vice President, and Secretary of Defense. The Security Council also has two special advisers: the chairman of the Joint Chiefs of Staff (which is part of the Defense Department) and the director of the Central Intelligence Agency (CIA). These two members give the council military advice and information gained by spies and other intelligence gathering. (The council also directs the general policies of the CIA.)

The United Nations

The United States Mission to the United Nations (U.N.) is also a section of the State Department, though it acts quite independently. The head of the

The United Nations building in New York City. The United States Mission to the U.N. is a part of the State Department.

Mission is the United States' ambassador to the U.N. in New York. He or she is also a member of the President's cabinet. Because of this, U.N. Ambassadors hold equal rank with the Secretary of State, even though the U.S. Mission is technically a part of the State Department.

Since both the Secretary of State and the U.N. Ambassador help form U.S. foreign policy, it's important for the President to pick two people who see eye-to-eye on these matters so that their decisions don't conflict.

The United Nations is an international organization that was formed shortly after World War II to keep peace and security around the world, and to maintain friendly relations among nations. It also tries to find solutions to worldwide problems like bad economies, cultural differences, and natural or manmade disasters. Making sure human rights and other freedoms are respected by all countries is also a big part of the U.N.'s job.

The United Nations replaced the League of Nations, which had a similar purpose but failed. "United Nations" was a name given by President Roosevelt in 1941 to describe the countries fighting against Germany and Japan in World War II. It was first used officially on Jan. 1, 1942, when 26 states joined in the Declaration by the United Nations. The new members pledged to continue their joint war effort and not to make peace separately. The official U.N. Charter was formed in 1945 at a conference held in San Francisco. Today the U.N.'s headquarters is in New York City.

Travel Help

The State Department gives passports to U.S. citizens who want to travel in foreign countries. Also, the State Department publishes several helpful books and pamphlets that give travelers tips on how to have a safe trip, as well as warnings when crises occur and travel is not advised. And when a U.S. citizen gets in trouble in a foreign country, the United States Embassy can offer help and protection.

Biographies

Thomas Jefferson

In 1790, George Washington wanted someone he could trust as the nation's first Secretary of State. He chose fellow Virginian Thomas Jefferson, who had already served his country well during the War for Independence. Jefferson organized the State Department, putting it on the right track for future secretaries, despite a very small budget.

Jefferson was born in the Virginia countryside in 1743. His father died when the young Jefferson was only 14. Thomas Jefferson inherited a lot of property, but the thing he valued most was his father's wish that his son get a good education. Jefferson went to college and law school, and soon learned that studying law was a good way to learn about society and its history, culture, and morals. With his schooling complete, Jefferson entered the Virginia colonial legislature (the lawmakers in charge while England still ruled America).

Jefferson became a leader in the fight for independence from England. He was called on to be the main writer of the Declaration of Independence. If this was all Jefferson ever did, America would be eternally grateful. But Jefferson's political career had just begun.

Jefferson became governor of Virginia in 1779. He guided his home state through the last years of the American Revolution. After the war, he was sent as Virginia's representative to the Continental Congress in 1782. (The Continental Congress was where the states made laws before there was a United States, or even a Washington, D.C. These would all come later, after the Constitution was approved in 1788.)

In 1784, Jefferson got his first taste of foreign service when he was sent by the Continental Congress to make treaties with France. He worked closely with Benjamin Franklin and John Adams.

Thomas Jefferson, our first Secretary of State.

Jefferson enjoyed his work as U.S. Minister to France. The job gave him a chance to put his many years of education and law experience to the test. He returned to America after five years of service.

In the fall of 1789, our first President, George Washington, asked Jefferson to become Secretary of State in our new government. Jefferson agreed, and in 1790 became one of America's first cabinet secretaries. As Secretary of State, Jefferson urged closer ties with France because he was suspicious of Great Britain. He was afraid that America's former colonial masters were trying to weaken the young United States.

Jefferson, of course, would later go on to become America's third President, serving from 1801 to 1809. He was the first president inaugurated in Washington, a city he had helped to plan.

After retiring from public service in 1809 at his beloved home, Monticello (which is shown on the back of today's nickel), Jefferson helped start the University of Virginia. He also continued his lifelong interests in science, architecture, philosophy, and the arts.

George C. Marshall

George C. Marshall served as Secretary of State under President Harry S. Truman. He was an American army officer and statesman. During World War II he helped direct Allied strategy and was named general of the army (a five-star general) in 1944. Because of his work raising and equipping military forces against the Germans, Winston Churchill called him "the organizer of victory."

As Secretary of State from 1947 to 1949, Marshall organized and directed the European Recovery Program (which was called the Marshall Plan). Marshall knew that the countries in Europe would need a lot of help recovering from the devastation left by World War II.

George C. Marshall, Secretary of State under President Harry S. Truman,
seen here in his U.S. Army uniform while a five-star general.

The Marshall Plan spent over $12 billion in American aid. Soon our allies in Europe were back in good shape. This served American interests as well, since strong friends are good friends.

In 1953 Marshall received the Nobel Peace Prize for helping rebuild Europe, as well as for promoting world peace and understanding.

John Foster Dulles

John Foster Dulles was probably the most powerful and controversial Secretary of State we've ever had. He served under President Dwight D. Eisenhower from 1953 until 1959, when illness forced him to resign. During his time as Secretary of State, Dulles was known as a strong negotiator who was firm in his belief that Communism must be stopped. He had a big part in forming our foreign policy during the height of the Cold War. Dulles had a very strong personality, and insisted on leading instead of following.

Dulles knew at an early age that he wanted to be Secretary of State. He knew how important the Secretary's job was, and wanted to help form America's foreign policy. He was a brilliant student. In law school he specialized in international law. Dulles served as the United States delegate to the United Nations from 1945-49. He negotiated the Japanese peace treaty that officially ended World War II.

As Secretary of State, Dulles emphasized the security of the United States and its allies through foreign economic and military aid. He also had to decide how to deal with Russia's obtaining of nuclear weapons. Dulles encouraged America to make nuclear weapons capable of "massive retaliation." His idea was that no enemy would launch a nuclear strike against us if they knew we would strike back with devastating total destruction.

With so much experience in international law, Dulles had a strong belief in the value of treaties. As a negotiator, he was very, very firm.

John Foster Dulles, Secretary of State under President Dwight D. Eisenhower from 1953–59.

(Many say Dulles was too stubborn.) He was a deeply religious man, and this was a big reason why he hated Communism so much. (The Communists in the Soviet Union outlawed religion.) Dulles seemed to get pleasure out of pushing the Soviet Union to the edge of crisis. He used to say, "if you are scared to go to the brink, you are lost." During crises Dulles firmly stood his ground, and the Soviets usually gave in.

Many people said (and still say today) that Dulles was a harsh, stubborn, and inflexible Secretary of State. They thought that instead of forming a broad, international policy for America, Dulles simply went from one crisis to the next. They thought that with his forceful personality he was a dangerous man to be at the head of the State Department. But Dulles' boss, President Eisenhower, ignored his critics. He called Dulles "one of the truly great men of our time."

Dulles was forced to resign in 1959 because he was very ill with cancer. Before his death, he was awarded the Medal of Freedom, the highest honor for a civilian in this country.

Henry Kissinger

Henry Kissinger served as Secretary of State from 1973-77 under Presidents Richard Nixon and Gerald Ford. Kissinger was an expert in international affairs and nuclear defense. As National Security Adviser, he had more influence over the President then Secretary of State William Rogers, Nixon's first Secretary of State.

Kissinger arranged for Nixon's historic trips in 1972 to China and the Soviet Union. He also negotiated with North Vietnam to end the war in Southeast Asia. (For this, he and North Vietnamese Representative Le Duc Tho received the 1973 Nobel Peace Prize.)

Henry Kissinger, Secretary of State from 1973–77 under Presidents Richard Nixon and Gerald Ford.

In 1973-74 Kissinger took many trips to the Middle East to try to get Israel and the Arab nations to talk peace. This "shuttle diplomacy" eventually paid off. Tensions in the area were eased. This led to the United States resuming diplomatic ties with Egypt and Syria. After President Nixon's resignation in 1974, Kissinger stayed on as Secretary of State under President Gerald Ford.

Kissinger talking with King Faisal of Saudi Arabia during a shuttle diplomacy trip to the Middle East.

Warren Christopher

In 1993 Warren Christopher joined President Bill Clinton as his Secretary of State. Christopher is known as a discreet and very strong negotiator. He has a lot of experience from his days as the second-in-command in the State Department under President Jimmy Carter. During those years, Christopher used to say, "Never get mad, except on purpose." In 1980 he played a big part in gaining the freedom of the 52 American hostages held in Iran. He also focused a lot of his attention on human rights issues and the Panama Canal Treaty. (After hard and lengthy talks, the United States turned over the Canal Zone to Panama in 1979, and agreed to give Panama control of the canal itself in 1999.) President Carter called Christopher "the best public servant I ever knew." Carter gave him the Medal of Freedom, the nation's highest civilian honor.

Christopher has humble beginnings, growing up in North Dakota during the Great Depression. His father died when the young Christopher was only 13. Christopher eventually went to school, got a law degree, and found himself in Los Angeles working for the law firm of O'Melveny & Myers. In the 1950's he led a letter-writing effort fighting against Senator Joe McCarthy. (McCarthy was a U.S. Senator from Wisconsin who abused his power as a senator by calling his enemies "Communists" and disgracing them, even if it was untrue. After the Senate condemned his actions, McCarthy's influence declined.)

Christopher has a long record of public service. He worked as Deputy Attorney General during Lyndon Johnson's presidency, and acted as Deputy Secretary of State under President Carter. In the 1980's, during the Reagan-Bush years, Christopher helped build O'Melveny & Myers in Los Angeles into one of the most successful and aggressive law firms in the country. Today, as acting Chairman of the firm, he is very well respected in Los Angeles. After the Rodney King beating controversy in 1992, Christopher headed a commission that looked into the Los Angeles Police Department. Horrified at the racism he uncovered within the police force, Christopher said that Police Chief Daryl Gates must leave. It was a hard decision that took guts to make. Gates eventually did leave.

In 1992, candidate Bill Clinton asked Christopher to help him pick a vice president. Christopher advised that the future president choose Al Gore, the U.S. senator from Tennessee. Together, Clinton and Gore swept into power on a promise of change from the business-as-usual climate of Washington, D.C. To help the transition, Clinton again came to Christopher, asking for help in choosing the best people to help the President run the country. Clinton was so impressed with Christopher's background, plus his cautious but firm negotiating style, that he asked him to be his Secretary of State.

As President Clinton's chief adviser on foreign matters, Christopher has a lot of hard work ahead of him. In the Middle East and Eastern Europe, especially, there are many difficult decisions to be made. One of Warren Christopher's heroes is George C. Marshall, who served as Secretary of State under President Harry S. Truman. Marshall did a great job in dealing with the troubles in Europe left over from World War II. Christopher now has a similar responsibility, since the fall of Communism left much of Europe once again in chaos and uncertainty. In early 1993 Christopher told President Clinton to move carefully in dealing with the crisis in Bosnia, to not send in our armed forces too soon. His influence with the President so far (as of mid-1993) has kept us mostly out of a war that would be incredibly difficult for any country to win.

Besides dealing with international crises, Christopher has another pressing concern in the State Department: making sure our embassies around the world help United States business compete for sales, contracts and investments. During his confirmation hearings in the Senate, Christopher said, "There has been this long tradition in American embassies that they prefer political issue . . . to assisting American businessmen, and I think we have to change that concept."

Warren Christopher, Secretary of State under President Bill Clinton.

Christopher also said that our embassies shouldn't be "shy or bashful about rolling up their sleeves and getting in and helping" when companies from the United States have trouble in foreign countries. If Christopher succeeds, then America should be better able to compete in a very tough world marketplace.

Warren Christopher has a strong belief in quiet, firm diplomacy. Although not shy about using force when absolutely necessary, Christopher has faith that most international crises can be settled by compromise. Whether or not he succeeds is for history to decide.

Secretary of State Warren Christopher with President Bill Clinton and Vice President Al Gore.

Glossary

Ambassador
A diplomatic official of the highest rank appointed as representative in residence by one government to another.

Cabinet
A body of persons appointed by a chief of state or a prime minister to head the executive departments of the government and to act as official advisers.

Cold War
The power struggle that arose between the United States and the Soviet Union shortly after World War II.

Communism
A system of government that controls the means of production. A single, party (like a dictatorship) holds power with the intention of making a better society in which all goods are equally shared by the people.

Congress
The national legislative body of the United States, consisting of the Senate and the House of Representatives. This is the place where laws get made.

Constitution
The system of laws and principles that guide countries on the nature and limits of government. The U.S. Constitution took effect in 1789. It establishes a federal republic with power balanced between the national government and the states. Within the national government, power is separated among three branches: the Executive (President), legislative (Congress), and judicial (Supreme Court). The U.S. Constitution is the supreme law of the land; no other law, state constitution or statute, federal legislation, or executive order can operate in conflict with it.

Diplomacy

The art or practice of conducting international relations, such as negotiating alliances, treaties, and agreements.

Embassy

The official headquarters in a foreign country of an ambassador and support staff.

Foreign Policy

How a country deals with other countries. Deciding to treat Country A as a friend and Country B as an enemy is a foreign policy.

Founding Fathers

The original group of men who decided what kind of government our country would take after the War for Independence.

Humanitarian Aid

Money and supplies given to a country's citizens because of terrible problems it cannot solve without help, such as famine or war.

Passport

An official government document that certifies the identity and citizenship of a person and grants permission to travel to a foreign country.

Superpower

A powerful and influential country, especially one with nuclear power that dominates its allies.

Treaty

An agreement between two or more countries.

Connect With Books

Acheson, Patrician C. *Our Federal Government: How It Works*. New York: Dodd, Mead & Company, 1984.

The Concise Columbia Encyclopedia on CD-ROM. Microsoft Corp., 1992.

Cunliffe, Marcus. *The American Heritage History of the Presidency*. American Heritage Publishing Company, 1968.

DeGregorio, William A. *The Complete Book of U.S. Presidents*. New York: Dembner Books, 1984.

"The Flint Beneath the Suit" *The Economist*. February 13, 1993, p. 30.

Gilfond, Henry. *The Executive Branch of the United States Government*. New York: Franklin Watts, 1981.

Howe, John R. *From Revolution Through the Age of Jackson*. Englewood Cliffs, New Jersey: Prentice-Hall, Inc., 1973.

Keatley, Robert. "Can an Old State Department Learn New Trade Tricks From Clinton's Man?" *The Wall Street Journal*, Jan. 22, 1993, pA7.

Parker, Nancy Winslow. *The President's Cabinet and How It Grew*. HarperCollins Publishers, 1991.

Sullivan, George. *How the White House Really Works*. New York: Scholastic, 1990.

The United States Government Manual 1991/1992. Washington, DC.: Office of the Federal Register, 1991.

Index

Adams, John 7, 16
Articles of Confederation 9
Bush, George 13
Carter, Jimmy 25
Christopher, Warren 25–28
Clinton, Bill 5, 25–28
Committee for Foreign Affairs 7
Committee of Secret Correspondence 7
Department of Foreign Affairs 9
Dulles, John Foster 20–22
Eisenhower, Dwight D. 6, 20–22
Foreign Policy 6
Ford, Gerald 22–24
Foreign Service 11
Franklin, Benjamin 7–8, 16
Gore, Al 26
Jefferson, Thomas 16–18
Johnson, Lyndon 25
Kissinger, Henry 9, 22–24
League of Nations 15
Marshall, George C. 18–20, 26
McCarthy, Joe 25
National Security Council 12–13
Nixon, Richard 9, 22–24
Passports 15
Rogers, William 9, 22
Roosevelt, Franklin Delano 15
Shuttle Diplomacy 24
Truman, Harry S. 26
United Nations 14–15
United States Ambassadors 11–12, 15
United States Constitution 4, 9
Washington, George 16, 18